M.C.
Here's a treat for you
to share with all your bikin
buddies ! Ride Free —

Miguel
7/7/91

THUNDER IN THE HILLS
Sturgis at 50

PHOTOGRAPHS BY MIGUEL LUIS FAIRBANKS

Introduction by Live Cheap-Never Die

OFF
THE
EDGE
PRESS
SANTA CRUZ, CA

Cover photo: *Electro-glide, Black Hills, South Dakota*
Title page photo: *Rolling down Main Street, Sturgis*

First Edition

Copyright (c) 1991 **OFF THE EDGE PRESS**
Photographs (c) 1991 Miguel Luis Fairbanks
Text (c) 1991 Live Cheap-Never Die
Printed by Pioneer of Jackson Hole, Jackson, Wyoming
Book design by Ted Wood and Barbara Rogers
Edited by Ted Wood

Library of Congress Catalogue Number 91-90271
ISBN 0-9629521-0-9

Published by
OFF THE EDGE PRESS
P.O. Box 37
Santa Cruz, CA 95063-0037

Dedicated to my mom, Bibi, who first introduced the magic of Harleys to my family; and to my aunt, Marguerite, whose spirit lives on in my heart.

Bibi in 1925

FOREWORD

by Miguel Luis Fairbanks

My fascination with Harley-Davidsons and the people who ride them goes back some time. As a photojournalist, I have repeatedly found myself attracted to those people who have the courage to buck the status quo. In essence, non-conformists. Bikers are such people. I consider myself such a person. Thus, it was natural that I should gravitate toward the culture and mystique that is Harley-Davidson.

But it wasn't until 1989, while cruising through the Santa Ynez Mountains near Santa Barbara, that I first heard of Sturgis. I had stopped to photograph a biker and his lady who were pulled off the road. "Going to Sturgis next summer?" he asked. "It's the 50th anniversary, and they say 400,000 bikers are coming." My mind raced. Nearly half a million strong! Where else *could* I be in August, 1990.

That summer, with some bikers out of Ocean Shores, Washington, we made the run to Sturgis, and my heart was captured. At the most basic level, the Sturgis 50th was for me an endless stream of great experiences, laughs and fine people. On a more profound level, I felt the spiritual connection one makes with people whose lives are based on a foundation of honesty, individuality and integrity. It may not be pretty at times, but you always know what you're getting. I'll take "real" over "nice" any day.

All the people I met were refreshingly non-judgmental (except towards yuppies). Their lives seem to transcend both image and convention. Bikers don't pretend; they are staunch allies to those who also have the courage of their own convictions. Most people don't see that the biker is one of the last, strong links to the founding principles of our country.

My photos and this book are about the individuals who embody those principles. My aim was to capture Sturgis as it happened, and I hope these images portray the great lust for life and freedom in the hearts of bikers. This is a tribute to them, the people who ride those thundering machines. May they show us all the art of being real, of being ourselves.

INTRODUCTION

by Live Cheap-Never Die

DOING IT STURGIS STYLE

In the summer of 1990, they said it would happen. And it did. A thundering tribe came from every direction, gawked at by curious onlookers for hundreds of miles. For a week in August, freedom roared through Sturgis, South Dakota, for the 50th anniversary of the Black Hills Motorcycle Classic, bringing together a curious brotherhood of men and women from all over the world.

What a week! A British lady working the desk at the Sturgis hospital declared she was leaving town for the week. The bikers could rape the place without her being there, she said. An 82-year-old woman, also a town resident eating in a restaurant filled with bikers, declared she loved them all. She wished she could still ride the way she used to.

The tribes have gathered in the Black Hills for centuries. Indians, gold miners, gamblers, outlaws, lawmen, missionaries, merchants — you name it, they all returned for the 50th bash. Local Sioux, foreign clubbers, rival motorcycle clubs, bikers for Christ, Blue Knights, Alcoholics Anonymous riders, old riders, kids and barking dogs. As usual, there were some who lived through it and a few who didn't. Some left with their pockets full of other people's money, and some pulled out with pawn tickets instead of the leather and knives they came with.

Moving anywhere near Main Street in the town of Sturgis was slow work that week. Traffic was thick. Even the thin coat of hot tar oozing up to cover the new pavement didn't thin out the unending arrival of motorcycles. You could hear tar sticking to the tires and feel it sucking at your feet. The sidewalks were too crowded to hold everybody, so this year the cops let people brave the tar path between rows of parked bikes. Trash glued itself to the sticky street. Each morning, before the tar heated up, you could get yesterday's news by standing in the middle of Main Street and reading the papers embedded in the pavement.

You read that the one guy the cops killed up the street yesterday with only nine shots was from Australia — a crazed citizen on drugs. What about the shooting and knifing at Gunner's Lounge? No papers carried that one. And how long would I have to wait in line to take a leak today?

Madness strikes Sturgis.

Fortunately, all around Sturgis the Black Hills smile down. Madness has come and gone before. Gold fever, Jesus pushers, land grabbers, blood hatred — just about any kind of man-made fetish that a soul can create has made the rounds in these hills. But it all evaporates once a person loses himself in the twists and turns of the magical Black Hills. As fast as a biker can wind his way through the canyons, mountains and plains of South Dakota and Wyoming, sanity and happiness return.

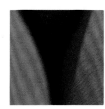

If madness was what people expected to find at the 50th in Sturgis, they weren't disappointed. The crazies work to keep things sane, and if it gets destructive now and then, that's the price to be paid. But the Hills haven't been destroyed yet. And neither have the brave souls who ride the highways.

"Where do they all come from?" Riders of Harley-Davidson motorcycles always hear this question when they travel to a meeting place like the Black Hills. People along the way to Sturgis had a right to ask this question in August of 1990. The supply of motorcycle riders seemed endless. Estimates ranged from 300,000 to nearly a million. It's hard for some people to imagine that so many men and women are actually like these people or would like to be in the same place with them. Why are they? Why would they? Where do they come from?

They come from everywhere. Take the distinguished so-and-so that I ran into last year in the Black Hills. I won't mention his name because we wouldn't want the potential for snobbery to ruin the man. Let's call him Red. Now I knew for a fact Red was a biker when I first saw him, because when he passed me on a 1937 Harley Flathead going uphill out of Deadwood (and I wasn't going slow), he was grinning too hard to be normal. Also, I knew he wasn't a youngster because when he showed me his teeth in passing, they almost ended up on the road before popping back into his mouth. The day was dry and hot, the sky was crystal blue, and I was cruising about two feet off the ground when I saw this bike pulled over on the roadside ahead. It was the same bike that had passed me. The guy on it was turned around and pointing to his back tire. I pulled over. That was the first time I met Red.

Red and I traveled our separate ways during the Sturgis rally. But more often than not, he and I would end up in the same place. During the time I spent with him, I became curious about Red. He had done himself the favor of having become a well-educated person. In the process he had acquired a style not like any you'll find again, because it was his own. He had earned it.

Red had started his trip from Los Angeles 2,000 miles away on his Hardtail with his son on the back. He'd always promised to take his kid on this trip to the Black Hills. Sometimes Red had money and sometimes he didn't. He said that there had been times when he'd had his pick of any bike he wanted to ride to Sturgis. This year Red only had enough money to get there, so that's what he left with.

By the time I ran into him, Red had $20 his brother had given him after he hit Deadwood. He had work lined up for the Sturgis rally, and prospects for the next night if he could get back from Hot Springs by eight to work the door at a Deadwood bar. Red's rear tube had developed a leak on the trip up from L.A. Now, the patch he'd fixed it with had ripped at the edge. I took 10 of his 20 dollars and headed back to Deadwood for a new tube and a Coke for Red.

I didn't return with a new innertube. There weren't any in Deadwood. So I got the patch patched, bought a can of fix-a-flat, a Coke and headed back the 20 miles to see how Red was doing under his shade tree.

Here was a set-up you don't run into every day; most people avoid uncertain circumstances. Red had started a trip a lot of people would never have considered. He was on a bike that only a few people even ride around town, much less 4,000 miles with confidence.

Well, a certain amount of concern was starting to show on Red's face the next night when I met him again at the #10 Saloon in Deadwood. Red didn't make it to the bar in time to get the job at the door. His tire had gone flat on him three more times that day on the way back to Deadwood. He was down on cash and short on supply.

I can't tell you how Red solved his finance problems. I can't say anything about his old drinking problems either, but I do know he sweats like an old-time boozer. Someone with style, someone like Red, doesn't worry so much about trouble and loss, because he carries the ability inside him to allow change to create new surprises for him. He's learned the advantages of not getting nailed down by his own limitations. Like he said, "Anything can be an adventure."

So watch someone who has a problem, where they must adapt to changes being dumped on them, and see what happens. While one person is anxiously trying to bolster up his reputation and past accomplishments, the person with style, an educated person, is still enjoying what is around him and is curious about what new opportunities will present themselves. I saw this happening at Sturgis. Red's only problem was that he had no money. But he arrived with his wits and his abilities intact. I saw another person arrive with a truck-load of goods to sell and a bankroll of bills to substitute for confidence. For fear of not making a large enough profit selling merchandise to bikers, this merchant was in a constant state of misery and spread it around to anybody who came near. On the other hand, Red managed a few business deals, met people, rode his bike and had a good time. People profited from Red's arrival. So did he. No one can say that for the merchant.

You acquire style from letting unexpected events pull it out of you. It's in you. It costs nothing. But you have to put up with inconvenience to get at it. Sometimes falling into the pit isn't as bad as staying out of the pit. As a group, bikers are often perceived as people who fall into one pit or another for as long as their health or the law will allow. But the idea that bikers have broken loose from normal society and are headed into the pit is only partly true. Many avoid dirt on their bikes in as worried a way as they avoid compromising situations. As a result of playing it safe, they stay clean; they never put their character on the line long enough to test it and give it a luster. An old biker once said, "You can ride a million miles, but if you never take a dirt road once in a while, you won't get anywhere." A motorcycle provides a good education because things can get at you.

Things get to bikers at Sturgis. An invisible thread joins the spirits of motorcyclists, as enduring as the natural strength of the Black Hills they come to share every summer. And when the call goes out from the soul of the land, there are souls of men and women who respond with the roaring sound of freedom. Be it violent or peaceful, the Black Hills will always be there to greet them.

Freedom calling
Hwy. 85 to Mt. Rushmore

West Coast International Ride
I-90 overpass

Asleep at the wheel
I-90 eastbound

Dreams of adventure
Greybull, Wyoming

"I started this ride back in '87 with 27 riders. It's always been an exhilarating experience, but leading 650 bikers to the Sturgis 50th was beyond words. It gave me a true sense of freedom and pride in our heritage."
Linda Peavy
HOG Tales editor

Westbound from Milwaukee

15

Roadside attraction

"It's just about impossible for a woman to come to a thing like Sturgis and not show a little skin."
                              Chloë Warren

Drive-in motel

"I've been to Sturgis every year since 1979, but this is the first time we stayed in a motel. I kinda liked it, you could sleep." Dan & Cathy Milbradt

17

Electro-glide
Black Hills, South Dakota

A motorcycle is a good education because things can get at you. The weather, cars, trucks and the pavement. In becoming educated, if you don't let anything get at you, nothing sinks in. And if nothing sinks in, you never fill up...

...And if you never fill up, you drain away to nothing. So when it comes to the land and its people, it pays to be traveling in a way that things can get at you. Sometimes you get hurt, but you forget the garbage. — *Live Cheap-Never Die*

The Wave
Buffalo Chip Campground

Roughing it
KOA, Gillette, Wyoming

Road weary
Hog Heaven Campground

Moonrise over Buffalo Chip

"Teepees are pretty comfortable livin' quarters, really. There were seven people inside and room for a couple more."

Tony & Rhonda Klein

Buffalo Chip Campground

Just married, I-90

*"I just got one little spot of grease on the
dress. Other than that, it held up pretty
good."*   Sue & Mark Langenfeld

The gathering
Main Street, Sturgis

"Can't say I remember the first one, but I've been here 92 years, so I've seen all the rallies. The bikers come and go. They don't bother us, really."

Christine Arnott, 92

Downtown Sturgis

YMCA Dairy Queen outing
Main Street, Sturgis

Illegal docking
Rapid City, South Dakota

The rare fur-bearing Harley

"I race him (Harvey Wallbanger). He's only lost 13 races out of 92 against quarter horses, thoroughbreds, and trotters."

T. C. Thorstenson, owner & jockey

1914 Harley-Davidson, twin chain
Main Street, Sturgis

Malcolm Forbes' Harley balloon
Rapid City, South Dakota

35

Rat bike

"When someone asks, 'What year is your bike?' I say, 'What part are you talking about. It's a 1929–1960 Harley-Davidson WL, depending.' "   *Junky Jim Fisher*

Spare tires
Sturgis exit, I-90

Car wash, Sturgis

"Our women don't understand the
relationship between a man and his machine.
It's not just a motorcycle; it's my freedom."

Mike Knowles, with Lisa

Hardtail
Main Street, Sturgis

Bones & Cheree

*"The studded leather and lace top made
me feel like Hollywood came to Sturgis,
except in Hollywood, people get worse with
age. I just get better."*   *Cheree McCoy*

"I made the top, bottom and chaps out of elk hide. In fact, you can still see the bullet hole in it. I don't usually act like this, but Sturgis makes me feel sensual."

Melana Whitaker

Sturgis formal wear

41

Hospitality tent, Covered Wagon Resort

*"Debbie and I met during the Sturgis
50th. It was a rally romance."*
Rick Rideout, Vietnam vet

Eye of the storm

"We just sat back and watched everyone partying down at Buffalo Chip. Chicks were getting naked and everything."

Jon Orth & Maureen Hand

Whoops, wrong turn

"When we made our reservations three
months ago, they never told us we'd be
next to a Harley convention."

The Hoffus Family, KOA, Rapid City

Royal Palace Restaurant, Cody, Wyoming

"We're kind of stuck in a time warp. We're like outcasts. We should have been living in the Pony Express era."

Cheryl Stengrund, with cat-eye glasses

The Great R. J. Rosini
Gypsy tattooer

Makin' Chorizo
Main Street, Sturgis

Hoggie Man

"Wearing the hog nose and ears was just something me and my friends started doing at HOG rallies."

"I lost a brother and a real close friend in Vietnam. I did the tattoos and gas tank to remember them. My brother was only 19."
Richard Hoggie Man Hunsucker

Crusader
Main Street, Sturgis

Snakin' through the Hills
Main Street, Sturgis

Fast Eddie & friends

"The thing about my friends is you can trust 'em with your bike, your woman and your life, and they won't fuck with any of 'em."   *Fast Eddie Lewis*

"He would have ridden a Harley."
Christian Motorcycle Assoc. pamphlet

Morning prayer service
Grace Lutheran Church, Sturgis

Dangerous curves ahead
Main Street, Sturgis

Yuppie cocktail party
Buffalo Chip Campground

The Texas Bandidos
Main Street, Sturgis

Eden revisited
Rushmore Plaza Civic Center, Rapid City

UFO Harley
On the road to the Buffalo Chip

Shooting at Gunner's Lounge
Main Street, Sturgis

Tiny, Hell's Angel
Main Street, Sturgis

Culture clash
Gunner's Lounge, Sturgis

Ear-deep in fur

"It took me three hours to shove my
helmet up that raccoon's ass."
Steven Scott & Sparky the helmet

Beer stop
Silver Dollar Bar, Cody, Wyoming

Tying the knot

*"Sturgis is not a 'follow the rules' scene.
So we decided to do something rad and
get married on stage at the Buffalo Chip."*
Charlie & Eve Morgan

Head-over-heels
Margaret Sutton & Gary White

Contestant #1
Miss Nude Buffalo Chip Contest

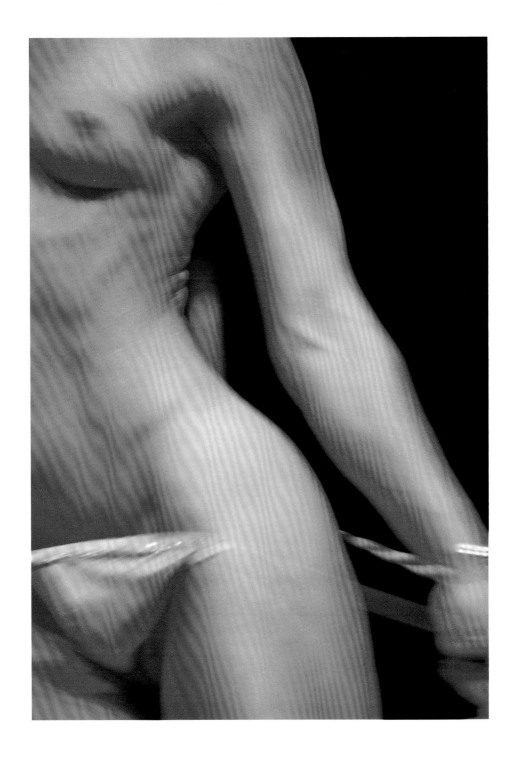

Contestant #2
Miss Nude Buffalo Chip Contest

Puss 'n Boots
Miss Nude Buffalo Chip Contest

Working the crowd
Miss Nude Buffalo Chip Contest

Panel of judges
Miss Nude Buffalo Chip Contest

Wild thing
Buffalo Chip Campground

Gregg Allman
Rushmore Plaza Civic Center

600cc races
Jackpine Gypsies' track, Sturgis

600cc winner, Chris Carr
Jackpine Gypsies' track, Sturgis

Nine Toes crashes the Wall of Fire

*"We use a gallon of gas on each wall,
which burns at 600° F. Actually, I don't
like fire at all. I've been burned bad twice."*

Nine Toes

"When I was 15, I got hit on my bike. I lost the big toe on my left foot. The toe portion of the boot was torn right off, including the sole."
Nine Toes Doug Marble

Two Machine Pyramid
Seattle Cossacks

Shoulder Dive and Bridge
Seattle Cossacks

Blast-off
Harley races, Sturgis Dragway

Sha Na Na
Rushmore Plaza Civic Center

Neon nights
Cody, Wyoming

Dresser Light Competition
Rushmore Plaza Civic Center, Rapid City

Superman rat bike
Main Street, Sturgis

Down for the count

"I met one guy from Norway and some others from Australia. We spent all night drinkin' Everclear, spittin' fire and toastin' to Crom, the Norse God of Steel."   L. B. Albro

When Harley riders ride together, it's not hard to
feel the presence of the power of freedom that
enticed warriors to the round table at Camelot,
or likewise pirates and sailors to a life on the
open sea, and horsemen to the American West...

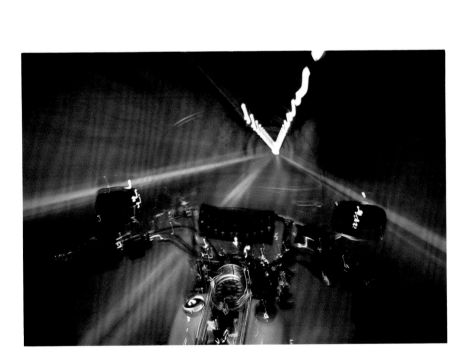

...Honesty before goodness. That's what biking is. Honesty in relating to your bike and to the people. Biking doesn't represent an image. It represents individuality, the freedom of the spirit, in all it's forms. — Live Cheap-Never Die

On the road again
Leaving Sturgis

ACKNOWLEDGMENTS

As with any great and worthwhile project, the goals cannot be achieved by the efforts of a single person alone, but rather require the inspiration and dedication of many people working toward a common vision. This project is no exception.

To begin, I extend my sincerest thanks to the wonderful people whose photographs appear on these pages, for without their good-humored compliance, there would simply be no pictures. They allowed me the honor of entering their lives and capturing a bit of their spirits to share with others.

Also, I would like to thank David McAllister, Tony Anderson, Janet Morgan, Russ Spooner and my brothers Carlos and Alden. They provided their time, expertise, moral support, insight and rides throughout.

But, my deepest gratitude I reserve for two people in particular.

First, I would like to thank my dear friend Ted Wood, who is not only my partner in crime, but also in *OFF THE EDGE PRESS*. Ted took the raw material of my photographs and created a dream for us. To that end, he imparted form, direction, vision and humor to this great book project, and thus transformed that dream into reality. Ted, I cannot thank you enough buddy.

Finally, I would like to acknowledge Chloë Marie Warren, one of the dearest friends to grace my life. Chloë went to Sturgis with me and in fact, worked at least as hard as I did, slept less than I did (if possible), and smiled and laughed throughout. Chloë drove 3,000 miles, fed us, assembled our tent, washed our clothes, ran for more film, held the flash, metered the light and pushed me when I wanted to collapse. It was because of Chloë's dedication that I was able to shoot 225 rolls of film in 10 days — it would have been impossible otherwise. And with great pride I watched her drive David McAllister's scooter 60 miles through Yellowstone. But most importantly, I thank Chloë for helping teach me to be free. That is the greatest gift of all.

Chloë, I adore you.